STFU
Pronounced
SI-TU-FU
PSW
POETRY SPOKEN WORD

NOCA PUBLISHING (NOCAP)

STFU
Si-Tu-Fu
PSW
POETRY SPOKEN WORD
©**Copyright 2023**
Nocapublishing [NOCAP]

ALL RIGHTS RESERVED
No portion of this Manual may be reproduced, stored in any electronic system, or transmitted in any form or by any means, electronic, mechanical, photocopy, recording, or otherwise, without written permission from the Author. Brief quotations may be used in literary reviews.

Cover Art by Intelligent Tarref Allah for Koozi Arts

-FOR BOOKINGS, INTERVIEWS, AND PUBLIC SPEAKING INFO-

Born King Allah
EMAIL: bornking7a@gmail.com

Printed in
The Wilderness of North America

STFU
Pronounced
SI-TU-FU
PSW
POETRY SPOKEN WORD

NOCA PUBLISHING (NOCAP)

Table of Contents

INTRODUCTION 3
FOREWARD... 4
MAKE NO MISTAKES 9
NOW FOUND 10
CHAINS... 13
BE ORIGINAL 15
CONCRETE JUNGLE 18
GOOD RIDDANCE 20
LOUDER THAN WORDS 23
OWN MY PAIN 25
CALL HOME 29
ON MY MIND... 31
KEYON I KING 33
BEST BORN 36
SOLID GOLD.. 37
YOU AND I 39
WORD IS BOND DAY 42
BLEEDING HEART 44
NOT HE.. 45
BLACK WISH 47
I LOVE YOU 48
USE ME.. 50
ANGIES POEM 51
YOU CARE 53
WISDOM GOD DAY 54
MS. YOU.. 55
SWEET MOTHER OF MINE MRS. P 56
BLEEDING HEART 57
HAPPY BIRTHDAY 59
PHYSICAL DAY 61
SWEET AS A ROSE 62
HEAD UP... 64
HINT... 66

BORN BLACK 68
CHOSEN FEW 70
TRAPPED BY SEX 72
FOR I AM THE GREAT THINKER 75
FREE THE LAND 78
MASTER OF THE GAME 82

Dedication

This book is dedicated to all my children and grandchildren. It is dedicated to my crazy biological Brooklyn born dysfunctional family. I discovered them after being here for 50 years. Shout out to Cousin Dan Pearson for making my Ancestry.com connection make sense. Through him I was able to reunite with my 2 little sisters and brother. Shout out to my sisters Carol and Phyliss and my brother Ellis. Later I got to meet my Aunt Shirley, her daughter Frizell, my cousin Martin Terry and my Uncle Mike during my visit to Bklyn.

To finally meet them was the event of a lifetime of seeking. It was a day I never thought would come but it did. To find out that my mother ship was right there in Starett City but still unable to acknowledge me was a brutal reminder. Everything does not have a happy ending. Some people don't want to be found.

The same way you can find people you can lose them as well. Everyone has a choice and you can't force love, or family. I have learned you can be a child without family and have children and still not be a family. My life is a living testimony to this fact. Let my pain be a learning experience. Let my joy be a lesson. Let this book be a guide through both and provide an exit from pain and an entrance into joy.

INTRODUCTION

PSW will be introducing the readership to people who have names but who for me were my muse's. At different periods in life we shared time and space that was memorable to me. It is those memories of them that inspired me to pick up my pen and write. Some of my Muses I've never seen, heard or even met in the conventional sense. I did meet her insides but never here on the outside. See she was the mothership connection that allowed me to touch down on this planet.
So to all who are mentioned if you happen to read this book and see your name let me say this. This book in no shape, form or fashion is meant to hurt you or your current relationship in any way possible.

Please accept my PSW as my healing process. This is how I dealt with both joy and pain as I traveled through both the light and darkness of my life.
To all my beautiful Black family both known and unknown I want to say I love you. Whether we are biologically, genetically, or just rooted together as Black people; we are still family.

I always said I was never going to be just a neighborhood God, Born King Allah is a universal God presenting a gift to as many of our family members as I can.
I am trusting that my STFU series is a gift you all can accept and gain something valuable from. Strap in and take the ride. **STFU PRESENTS PSW!**

FOREWARD

When writing many a time my mind seeks to establish a bond with the readership that connects them to my innermost thoughts. They cannot be heard or read unless I birth them verbally or through the pen which is mightier than the sword. What this means when I say it is this. My pen is mightier than the sword above the heads of people bound to oaths and obligations who cannot speak truth to power as my books do.

My pattern of thinking is not to be followed rather it is presented as history best rewarding those who take the time to research it. We live in a common era of lies, deceptions, shape shifters, identity thieves and those seeking to trade places with the original Blackman because he is the God of this planet.

Those currently ruling our Earth are white not Black who have created the illusion they are the God of this planet. They have created a world in which the right are made to appear wrong and wrong is made to appear right.

As Black men Allah blessed we have access to the 3rd eye that allows us to see all for what it is and not just what it appears to be. We are this era's all eye seeing despite the fact of the wicked mans ruler ship of it. As such is truth STFU PRESENTS PSW is absolutely necessary to humanize the Black God.

"I have said ye are all Gods and children of the most high but ye shall die like men and fall like one of the princes". Once the wicked man realized God was a living Blackman he sought to constantly kill us so we would die like men. Morally, idealistically and culturally he experimented with ways to make us fall like one of the princes. So God needs to be humanized again so the 85% can get their heads out of the white clouds of deceptions looking for God who is right here in the person of the Blackman on this earth.

That means we must remove God from the sky and put him back into his body so he can be seen and heard, walking and talking. This way we can re-introduce and teach those who don't know God in the flesh how to properly identify him.

Once God is properly introduced then we can teach people how to become self saviors and rise about the mental bondage denying them access to the reality of God. The greatest secret kept from the people in this era is that God returned to us in 1964 which is nearly 57 years ago. The same way Allah the God came to resurrect and save us the wicked came to destroy him for freeing us from the mental death we suffered at their hands.

So even though we saw his physical body die like a man, Allah still lives because we are the life force that is Allah in our flesh.

Allah had already raised us from the 85% grave yard of the living dead. We were already the chosen people of the Original Blackman God in the flesh who named us the 5%. However, Allah gave us all he had and all within his power as our Father of Civilization and God of the universe. So now for the third time we his 5% sons were reborn again this time like father like son.

As a result, we become the Blackman God A alike our Father Allah. In just a short span of 5 years he was able to successfully transfer the power over the sun moon and stars to us the true and living Gods he had had just born us to be. See Allah knew they were coming and since his plan was best Allah lives today in us and can never die because we are the forever people.

Many say art imitates life but we say life intimates art because living in any kind of world will bring forth expressions that mark that time or era of existence. Life for us is the intimate relationship of God with the cosmos and all things good and bad that exists within it.

How one is unaffected or affected by what we see, hear and digest sonically or visually can seep into our art. Some of us draw pictures with paint brushes and others use pens, wood, metal or sculpting.

Using these vehicles, we bring that which lies within us outside of our bodies so others may see what we are thinking. Art is the communication of your inner thoughts bought to life in the outer world for consumption by the eyes and ears of our fellow inhabitants of the planet. We have ideas that once materialized into whatever form of art we are proficient at constructing, brings benefits to those who observe it.

This second volume of STFU like the first is a directive for those who need to SHUT THE FUCK UP! We speak for and define ourselves and have done so for milleniums before those who don't know what they are talking about physically existed. I get it; you thought we were like a chalk board; A BLACK SURFACE YOU COULD WRITE YOUR WHITE CHALK LIES ON TO ERASE OUR ORIGINAL BLACK GOD IDENTITY. You thought wrong and as we observe signs and symbols of the primordial Black man to the signs and symbols of our art today we rediscover the truth.

We are the one and the same and directly connected to the root of this planet's civilization as the Original man of it. Your white presence is but a mere blip in the time that is present and we recognize you are not the gift you are the curse. We reject you now as did our wise ancestors who first met and rebuked you as the real devil you are. We come now in this period of your overtime to chronicle the fall of Babylon and modern day Sodom and Gomorrah. This is the era of the Roman Empire in all of its devilishment renamed and reborn as America twice as wicked and three times as corrupt.

This edition of STFU is completely different from the first edition. You will be able to laugh, cry and experience the joy and pain this Blackmans life experience has shown him. For this writer, poetry came first as it was the simplest way to give a gift that money couldn't buy.

I discovered Poetry was and is the intimate revelations of expressive vulnerabilities buried under the hardcore exterior of this man's man. The ability to get in touch with that Alive Real Truth (ART) within myself is the result of the keys Allah the father gave me to unlock the seven seals within myself.

I take everything from knowledge to born and whether you understand that or not just know I can teach you how to do the same. I have been able to take introspective journey's deep inside myself to discover new worlds of consciousness. As I became the lord of all my worlds I can now touch the conscious and subconscious as a enlightener to my readership.

For those of you that my STFU directives are the shoes that fit your feet, just know we have you right where we want you. The books you all have written proves you are liars in print being righteously brain spanked by the truth printed in STFU. You have now encountered the Black hand which is now slapping you in the face with truth. **WELCOME TO STFU PRESENTS PSW POETRY SPOKEN WORDS**

MAKE NO MISTAKES

If I had the chance to do it again
To reveal the truth that exists within
The world in this universe, we call home
I'd lock the devil up in the twilight zone
Cause he took too many lives and it was Black blood shed
How many more of us by his hands will lay dead
See the devil he works in mysterious ways
Sending devilishment and lies through the very air waves
Through the TV and radio waves of sight and sound
The devils thoughts have people held caught and bound
How much longer will this continue this invasion within our lives
With us his unknowing victims of his lies bullshit and jive
Well time is on our side in case you didn't know
Payday will arrive when he must reap what he has sowed
Now don't misunderstand me because the penalty's really death
The only real fit justice for just a dangerous pest
So to punish the real devil who deserves to get no breaks
Be extra special careful and please **Make No Mistakes!**

NOW FOUND

You know when I write it's like light, illuminations from my mind thoughts told made to unfold like magic, the pen is my wand and paper the canvas Bond for this teacher to speak and reach

The masses of the Blind, deaf and Dumb left mindless and violently out of touch with their own reality, so they grasp the straws that break the camel's back never getting over the hump of poverty economically so ironically the dead are fed before the living. Money collected for the Messiah 2000 years past and I am aghast because nutrition is not a steady diet of spoon fed lies.

But when will you and I the third eyed brothers not Blind be recognized as purveyors of the truth that shall set you free, instead of just another smooth talker New Yorker with a God complex… who figured out how to solve for X. Don't forget here is why we remain the best chance my people have to get back right by eating Black truth from our tree of life.

Tell me if you can why the knowledge of Ancients was given to the Babies and not the lazy crazy super rich sons of bitches in their mechanical armor. Y2k yesterday, today and tomorrow. I still feel the sorrow of my ancestors who swung from your ropes, I hate white folks and twine. We need to Bill Gates and Clinton for reparations pain and restitution and destroy the institution of neo slavery and creative racism. The bigger picture shows that they're both Micro soft creators of schisms and isms. Hollering not guilty for the Black Holocaust and though you think I am lost I still find you responsible. So compute this nothing can save you vengeance is mine saith the Lord.

The greatest trick the Devil ever pulled was convincing the world he did not exist, but ask my Indian brothers who resist if he is real or not, reservations. Check the plot Plymouth Rock... Guess who's coming to dinner made devils the winner. So every Nov 24th he celebrates his Thanksgiving with a Happy meal. We ponder how just like Jeffery Dahmer death was the main menu scalps were peeled and mass murder was the family deal. These devils are cannibalistic bastards at their root, who turned into captain caveman savages in business suits
Old McDonald had a farm where the pigs are armed in Philly on move they dropped their bombs. NYPD blue perverted advisory not observed. I heard A Volpe just inserted a plunger in the rectum of Abner Louima. Tell me not that I'm a dreamer for the horror I feel and see, death is the only real payment for a murderer such as thee. These Devils in blue suits are over privileged jocks with itchy trigger fingers bold enough to shoot Amadou Diallo 41 times to make sure he didn't live to get old. No reason given Our people are victims of I declare War on the Black Community. Government gives cops 007 immunity, giving them license to be our killers with impunity. They're Reinforcing Black genocidal continuity. Their Injustice systems hollers their pigs are not guilty but the world must be made to see our death at your hands can't be free. We're going to make them pay for their murderous crimes against Black Humanity.
So in conclusion I radiate unity fusion to repair the broken black family tree branches that have been denied access to the root. You see my seed becomes my fruit as it is stated. The Babies are the Greatest, so in my battle I must be brave for it is their lives that

I must save. Wise words spoken intelligence is my throne, when from the kingdom of God knowledge is made known.

To awaken Black masses and turn them around to the truth. In the beginning was the word, check my sound cause I'm freeing the people who for too long were bound. As it was written the words spoken are so profound letting everyone know there's a new sheriff in town. So people once lost have been **NOW FOUND**

CHAINS

They fit as tight as a bottles waterproof cap
They are the links that hold us securely in a trap
Oh please release us from this injustice and pain
Were the pleas of those amongst that were just all in vain
On the Good Ship Jesus a floating hellhole for men
Stacked one upon another just like animals in a pen
Kidnapped from our homeland we traveled stifled by our waste
Labeled $3/5^{ths}$ human when really were the ancient royal Black race
Free before the beginning but in the end we'd wind up sold
By savages from Europe who spouted lies so bold
They said it was their duty that they were ordained by God
To beat and kill us in the name of religion with the Bible and iron rod
So by the thousands did we suffer by the millions did we die
A Holocaust of mass proportions to this day we still ask why
But get no answers to the questions because truth is buried by lies
By the sons of the fathers who own a piece of the American blood pie
So the voices of my black ancestors speak loudly from their graves
Banish these pretenders to civilization back into their caves
They refuse us reparations as payment for their sins
They keep us isolated thinking if its just one on one they'll win

But we're the chosen people and this land we've built we'll own
We'll save it and ourselves from destruction slavery seeds have sown
So until this time of judgment Armageddon is the name
My people remain ruled by a tyrannical race that is criminally insane
Diabolical enslavers of my people egotistical killers for wealth and material gain
Black wrath is coming to punish you for putting us in mental and physical **CHAINS**

BE ORIGINAL

When all that is left is your hopes and dreams and your life flickers by on your memory movie screen then hold on tight, don't let yet your sword grow dull but most important don't be afraid to Be Original

In a world of copycat impersonators, followers and mentally dead you have to remain independent self-willed thinkers or you'll turn Frankenstein in the head. Living in your body with another man's brain is paramount to driving a car on the tracks of a train. So hold on tight, don't let your sword grow dull but most important Don't Be afraid to be Original

Roses that bloom in the gardens of life, have to be watered and receive sunlight. They have to be protected from weeds that seek to bring death, to every single plant seeking to draw breath. So must we be wary of the many who seek, to suck our life blood until we are crippled and weak. These Energy vampire creatures in all colors and shades, will experience the stroke of my double edged blade. And get impaled out of existence with a stake in the heart, see I stop weeds and vampires before their destruction starts. So hold on tight and don't let go but most important Don't Be afraid to be Original.

To stand up and say I know who I am, I'm Black I'm dominant a man amongst men. An individual personality who is grounded in truth, I touch it, I tell it, I shame the devil with proof. Of my existence in life it's simple and plain. The Blackman is God and Allah is my name. But for the chosen amongst us who acknowledge the same, are many who choose or fall victim to the game. Where for money, prestige, women or for fame, the players get played as loser's although winning was their aim. See the only success in being other then yourself, is the value of your stupidity in helping your enemy stack wealth. So hold on tight and don't let your sword go dull but most important Don't Be afraid to Be Original.

In the confusion of Chaos uncertainty and fear, arise like a phoenix bring order and stay clear. Of the curves in the road and people with forked tongues, walk steady on the righteous path and the battles half won. But intestinal fortitude is needed to solidify your goals, what profit a man who gains the world but loses his soul. So inner strength becomes the iron shaped and forged by adversities fires. That won't allow your intelligence to be superseded by your base carnal desires. Neither by emotions, immaterial to the relative world of Black men Black women, Black boys, and Black girls. So hold on tight and don't let your sword go dull but most important don't be afraid to Be Original

You see through my silence I have found my voice. The pen through written word silently screams my choice. Wisely chosen for tomorrow when today is past and gone, my words in print will eloquently speak my thoughts long and strong. Be wary of false prophets singing self praises proud and vain. Protect your brain from their nonsense that will yield you no intellectually relevant gain. But if by chance you must confront a lip professor face to face let him speak the words that usher in his own disgrace. The downfall of the foolish is that they're both ignorant and bold they'll take the truth then make a lie as deep as a six foot hole. They're Grave builders of negative thinking equaling death, brain snatchers of my people who must be put to rest. So hold on tight and don't let your sword grow dull but most important Don't Be afraid to Be original.

In a world of grafted people thoughts and ideas, we remain freedom fighters unchanged by doubts and fear. Of the enemy in our midst and what remains to be done, To antidote the poison fed our people to stop them from becoming one. Divide and conquer is the tactic he's got oreos on his crew. They're Black people on the outside but inside they're as white as Elmer's glue stuck to their mutant slave makers parroting their thoughts Thomas Sowell, Michael Meyers, and Roy Innis are race traitors whites have bought. So hold on tight don't let your sword go dull, but most important Don't Be afraid to Be Original.

Enlist in the people's army arm ma gedd him in this rumble, Mr. white American society will be the first cookie that crumbles. Know for a surety we're coming for your heads, but first the snakes amongst us pushing Oreo agendas will be dead. That will leave you no more agents to feed you our master plan. It's the day you've feared the most it's the revolution for the land.

For the people whose blood stained history has been pushed aside. By vile lazy imposters who have enjoyed a free ride. On the plane of hard work, ethics, and vast economic gain, we did all the work but received no credit for the same. So in essence free labors over and slavery is dead I'm on a mission hunting slavers and taking off their heads. For your philosophical religious chemical and germ warfare, you must be taken off the planet you can no longer live here. This earth just isn't big enough for us to co-exist in peace, so I've pulled the plug times up on your 6000 year lease. Its good riddance to the devils so Black people can live and teach the Blackman's God in the North South West and East. So hold on tight don't let your sword grow dull But most important Don't be Afraid...... **BE ORIGINAL**

CONCRETE JUNGLE

As I step out into the ghetto streets of the inner city slums
I stay on point cause down these streets the blood of my people runs
Black on Black crime is a problem a fact most everybody knows
But there's a hidden hand at work the TV cameras refuse to show
There's a method to this madness we see here in the hood
Orchestrated to make the good seem bad and all the bad seem good
You see the nucleus of this Nation has always been the backs of the poor
Disenfranchised who work for nothing because their needs always cost more
Then the jobs that never pay them the cost of food, clothes and rent
Creating an endless cycle of survival as we struggle with bills to make a dent
In a system and odds stacked against us to keep us a permanent underclass
We fight to live to make a home but death always finds us so fast
Subjected to all forms of warfare where our people are under attack
Liquor stores and churches on every corner given aids and drugs like crack
That helps this capitalist government secure their future by chemically enslaving Blacks
And since white hands are invisible for all societal ill it us who catch the flack
Look they do it to themselves so their spilled blood is not attached to our hands

Don't blame us for your troubles say their murderous Klu Klux Klan
Just one of the many militias controlled by the elite and super rich
Who hide behind many masks and faces to back us into a ditch
Or should I say a grave of poverty self ignorance and fear So the cry and pleas of inner city people fall upon deaf ears
But there's a generation arising immune to white peoples dirty tricks
We've unmasked these slimy wicked people who think that they're so slick
But the time has come to do battle no more genocide of our family tree
We're the warriors for the cause which is our Black people must be free
To protect our babies, we'll kill for Black justice and just Equality
That simply was never given so we are taking it and soon you'll see
Our people are in position as we chant rumble Black warriors rumble
Until we see the blood of our oppressors running in the streets of the **CONCRETE JUNGLE**

GOOD RIDDANCE

It was inevitable, but now it's due time
Good riddance to your ass your birth was a crime
Against my humanity, my pride and Black face
And so I had to kill you and murder was the case
That they gave me and I stand guilty as charged
I thought it would be easy but you fought real hard
You didn't want to leave this planet you call home
So you called on all the supporters you had ever known
First up the cracker bastard your Father in Slavery's name
Who formed your structure in his pea sized little brain
Next up jim crow institutions that validate your use
Along with your tools like racism, whips and a hang mans noose
And then there is his family his children and his wife
Recipients of white supremacy who thinks they're superior in this life
They used you brazenly in their songs, films and books
To denigrate, miss-educate and spread the hate you cook
Inside the melting pot they call the good old USA
That's actually nothing more than an organized KKK
So now like excrement is expelled you're expiring and decaying
Into a putridly pus filled entity destruction the price your paying
So that others can afford freedom from your blood sucker like existence
That was so subliminally seductive, you destroyed innocent people's resistance
So many fly guys and gals got caught by the deceit inside your web

Until they too became Frankenstein imposters your brain inside their head
Monstrous mutated creatures filled with alien thought
Existing with no substance or meaning foolish is their talk
They have no knowledge of self their history Nation or God
Products of the environment who reject intelligence in order to act hard
So they continue using sound to give life to your poisonous word dung That hits the ears of a lot of people with the force of a loaded gun
Creating new definitions while pushing common sense to the curb
Is as foolish as loving your enemy but some of us still have not heard
The fat lady whose singing is bringing all the good news
Of your end your demise and the birth of right views
True alternatives to identify the primordial of man
The first Born Original Black seed more countless than grains of sands
In the hourglass of time our people have had many a name
Black, Nubian, African, Moor but we're really all the same
Despite geographical differences here now is our claim
We're still one people with one purpose and one aim
To eradicate all opposition found in anyplace
Word to my people is simple up you mighty race
Past, present and on to the future we still remain historical figures
So you'll always be my brother but you've got to get bigger
Then that little 6 letter word that we had to put to sleep in a grave bed
By the same hands that put a crown of intelligence on top of the Blackmans head

So rock a bye bastard baby you'll sleep forever from gunpowder mixed with lead
We're hit men who pulled the trigger and our victim the N word now is dead
GOOD RIDDANCE

LOUDER THAN WORDS

Don't tease me with promises you know you won't keep
Like for instance I'll write you King like three times a week
Then let a month go past that number thirty one days
In which I received no mail not a word did you say
For the sake of cooperation and because father knows best
I accepted your apology and put my hurt away to rest
Received your assurances I thought I heard never again
But here in the month of September you seem allergic to pens
Or is it to paper or envelopes or maybe it's the stamps
Or perhaps you're now arthritic and your fingers catch cramps
But whatever your reason the result is no joke
If I get paid for attention I'd be stone cold broke
Being emotionally abandoned has shown me the truth
Face value means nothing only time borns the proof
If the words easily spoken can manifest the deed
Word is Bond, bond is life so we must forever take heed
Not to let time pass so fast that we'd no longer be able to see
That years, months and days must count for you and me
You see every day of our separation would be easier to bear
If you'd take 32 cent flights and travel from there to here
It's becoming painfully clear that at this point in your life
You have no time for me, cause you're too busy to write

So my response to your one letter sent in the last two months
I'm in prison not a monastery trying to become a monk
So this poem is my pain and my questions I know you've already heard
Despite your answers not coming your actions speak **LOUDER THAN WORDS**

OWN MY PAIN

Tell me who is that knows my pain and when you find him tell him I don't want to see him today for my yesterdays are full of his presence and presently I am striving to adjust. See pain came to me 39 years ago and stuck to me like Black on skin. It should be suffice to say he was an unwelcome addition but in the sad tradition of life time suffering he was there in the beginning.

Once upon a time three score and nine years ago a little Black baby Boy was born and I'm torn. There's a mystery surrounding exactly when but of course he'd like to thank the dick he rode on in. Some say it was Oct. 24th others say Nov. 24th but then again lets go to the source for the birth report... but of course the Mother ship is missing. So the plot thickens and years go by. Abandoned he is shuffled like so many cards in a deck until like a little pound puppy he is chosen because he is little and cute. You can dress him in suits name him and claim him as your clone but he was always his own...little person.

Only he felt the pain that internally scarred his precious little heart and turned his veins into ice cubes because of the lack of heat and love. This winter baby became cold blooded and unloved or unlovable. Incapable of returning feelings that were strangers to his emotional makeup kit and don't forget, don't bite the hand that feeds you.

Its time some measure of care was given but we take it for granted that since you're living that's expected don't we? Children's Aid. I mean where would we be as a society if no one cared for the foundlings extricated from the rubbish filled garbage cans of this country's cities. If an innocent defenseless baby does not command the compassion of those who have it all and give nothing where would we be? I think we would be right here in the Belly of America land of the free home of the Black ex slaves. You see it is on conquered land on which we have been forced to roam, non- citizens 3/5^{ths} scorned, homeless and worn but I digress, but back to the Black Baby Born

A commentary on the social ills and climate that denied mothers the opportunity like Drake to say "Hey give me a break"... and get it. So because she can't take care of herself and me too I was left to fend for myself. Oh Black woman if only you could know the depth of my pain and how my brain burns with the hurt fire when I say your name at the end I say liar.

For I was your womb child, and though your insides promised you would always be this baby's mother your outsides broke that promise in a 1000 pieces. Black woman as I grew the pain grew with me and so whenever I met anyone that looked like you I remembered and called them liars too.

No trust leads to the unconscious or conscious abuse of persons I would like to love but can't because you are unforgiven. You have not come forward to count the tears, console the fear and eliminate the years of suffering perhaps with one heartfelt kiss on my head and a solemn I'm sorry. Instead I have been forced to think that it was all my fault.

That I was too little, too Black, too real, to be the fantasy that shoved itself out from between your legs and screamed. Maybe it was my voice you could no longer stand, the; I need your breast milk demands. Or maybe it was the fact that I was a little son of man who reminded you a little too much of another man, my Father.

Maybe it was because I was an accident and when you waited 9 months and I happened to make it you just threw me away so you could get your shape back and shake that ass as an unencumbered by any children Black woman with no class. Looking for a date with Mr. Right who turned into Mr. Right now, I got it now I'm gone like the guy you hate and is it because he left you that you left me?

They say wrath has no fury like a woman scorned. So now the Black baby's torn, no mommy, no daddy, no family tree. Instead he's fallen into an abyss and there's no connecting the dots to get to who I am and how I came to be. There is only Pain and Me

The question must be asked and answered who are you? And I even now wonder how do I get back to you. The umbilical cord is long broken and there are no signs to follow.

Still I look for footprints in the sands of time, for I know as long as there is air to breath that it will never be too late for us to relate. For I think I know you inside and out, well that's another story but my eyes have seen the glory of the coming of our time to meet.

Visually in the recesses of my mind I see you but I can't hold you long enough to picture your face and remember your name...Mommy. But that I could have had the joy to say that word and live that life would pain still be the same? If by receiving your love would I have still turned into an empty vessel of dark brooding expression of everything but love? Or was your giving me away the ultimate selfless move on your part to help me know my name and **OWN MY PAIN**

CALL HOME

Some say the hearts just a muscle that simply pumps bloods

Others say it's care like the flowers that in springtime blossom and bud

But I know it's like the secret that's been hidden from man

And buried deep in the garden that we'll now call Loveland

I'll show you how to get there, one step at a time

Then you'll know the happiness of a feeling divine

If you've never been there this poem will give you clues

To discovering the path to lead you there we start with 1&2

That defies all description because it's new but sometimes old

Love has the power to conquer everything according to legends told

To us the cold and empty people searching wherever we might be

To uncover the greatest love of all deep inside of me

But then in order to keep it you must learn to give it away

Find a significant other and here's the words you must learn to say

Baby for me there is no other because I only love you

These feeling are yours to share because love is meant for two

It's a one on one connection because you love me back

You genuinely care, respect and love I know it's not an act

Here's the best kept secret that's worth it's weight in gold

That was buried deep in Loveland and discovered by one so bold

To trust her with love's muscle, put your heart inside her hand

Total trust given to a woman who loves and guards the hearts of man

Here's the best part we've both learned it's better to give than receive

But when she puts her heart in your hand tell her you'll never leave

So herein lies the secrets and steps to the path inside a poem

Cause love is a house but the heart is where love will always **CALL HOME**

ON MY MIND

In a picture perfect world your beauty would be in a frame
And like Rembrandt and Picasso all the world would know your name
But would it make a difference would our relationship still remain
Or would it be affected, changed and no longer be the same
Thinking of you I seek to touch that beating heart deep inside your chest
Through written word I remain close to a woman who is quite simply the best
I know the depth of your beauty and how it can't be denied
We live in a world that values feminine beauty that is beheld by eyes
So because now I can't see you but I know that others do
I sometimes feel threatened by others who like me are thinking of you
But I go on with my long distance courting of you my lady love
Allegorically speaking you're a hand and I'm your glove
Snug we fit together and you put me on when you get cold
So carry me in your heart as protection from men attempting to be bold
Who approach my earthly jewel with words that just don't fit
Like Johnnie Cochran said to jurors if it don't fit then they should quit
Cause ain't no power in this universe or even on this earth

That can stop the healing process witness the joy of loves rebirth
It's really something special that we share a one of a kind
Love that conquers all opponents and passes the test of time
And whether you get famous or I become world renowned
Our foundation has been built together you're the jewel and I'm the crown
So my thoughts of you inscribed in words written on these 24 lines
Are designed to bring you comfort and security because you're always **ON MY MIND**

KEYON I KING

In the flash of an instant by the tick of the second hand of a clock, I compute the change to come in sec, minutes and hours and see that they add up its time.

That which began in the beginning that never began is the infinite possibility of forever existence existentially exuding exemplifying the principles of Alpha and Omega for that which never started of course will never end.

You see I came through come to be the resurrection of the Complexion connected in Blackness to the Darkness of Universal substance my name is I am but yet I always was.

A first word was Be. Cee becoming was the Multiplication of thought traveling at a speed only Me Myself and I could detect, Until my collective became the Bio Nuclear atom basic building blocks for my structural Arm Leg Leg Arm Head. Behold the two headed one.

And so in the dawn of creation I am Born. Let the sun shine in because from Darkness came light and from Dawn came the Eve my Bio Chemical opposite of feminine gender proud possessor of the Micro Universal womb X man now called Woman

From I he came into she Queen, Moon, Mother, Earth of antiquity Bodily Bonded to me is she the recipient of my affection not just a fling. I am Born King Allah's A alike son let the moon reflect the light of the Earths and heavens bound sun.

The sun exists in the Solar system above magnifying

rays of life giving force upon 9 spinning in place planets perfectly positioned. One planet is poised to become the home, heaven, habitat for the Great God of Universal proportions near and far. I am Born King Allah. Let the Earth bear witness and receive

As it is above so it is below and so I descended and became a Celestial Terrestrial walking on Earth, Wind, Fire and water. The fundamental elemental piece with the Magnetic, First born son of Self. I master all Nature my simple name is Man, Twin of the sun second to none. Mathematically I am knowledge number one multiplied by infinity. Let time begin

For it was I who planted the seed of Life in the Core of Planet Earth so that she could become bountifully, blessed blooming bequeathing plants, minerals, animals, a veritable cornucopia of diversified Life forms.

My kingdom come Let my will be done

And behold the Majestic, Magnificent, Moral Ruler of all that can be measured. I sit on the throne of Judgment and by my side sits my feminine fountain of fertilized flesh soil in Earthly form my biological partner, my corresponding Principle in Nature its true. I remain the one but now she is Two.

Let the One and his Two make three for we must be fruitfully reproductive in the Genetic Replication of the Supreme Beings Body form we make love to the early morn and a star is born in one day though his birth is 9 months away. We marvel at what is now called sex opening dimensional doors to this world from the next.

In the flash of an instant by the tick of the second hand of a clock I the official keeper of time compute

34

the eons and ages and they add up to 24. Sure, being the life giver is a beautiful thing and who can measure the joy that a new son brings. His time is now to be greater than me his name now spoken is **KEYON I KING**

BEST BORN

The exceptional skills that I possess
My unique capabilities that kind of suggests
One of the greatest better than the rest
From the top to the bottom I dress to impress
I'm quite debonair with good looks I've been blessed
So now it is time to I admit nay confess
That all through my life I knew I was best
Destined for fame I wouldn't settle for less
A number one fella with a bullet proof love
Black woman I'm the God descended from above
To touch down on this planet it ain't no game
You'll call me every day, but Born King is my name
Putting words together to reach out and touch
You with real affection that you've missed so much
Words lead to actions that's the goal of my charms
Step to the heavenly shelter found within my arms
Let me take your body where it needs to go
Ecstatic pleasure from your lips down to your toes
Then just lay back while I whisper in your ear
I love you baby and I ain't going nowhere
I'm your forever lover I've got it going on
I've always been the man just because I'm **BEST BORN**

SOLID GOLD

The duality of loves existence is that sometimes there is pain
But there's a feeling called happy when out loud I utter your name
Beautiful Mei Earth Asya don't you know you're my life
We're soul mates forever first my lover now my wife
Bonded together we have decided to give
Ourselves to each other for as long as we may live
We make our decisions to build to be eternally blessed
With a life filled with happiness we minus the mess
And add positive input that includes our common sense
Because adversity is the enemy we are both up against
No matter the distance or who stands in our way
A love that's sunny has filled my days
It's not just at night that my dreams come true
I thought of a woman so you're mother birthed you
To fulfill my destiny to walk upon the land
With you as my woman and me your Black man
Remember how it was back when we first met
The attraction was there but I had yet to get
To the point that I saw you as my dream in the flesh
But I knew you were special, I wanted to hear yes
To all of my questions Ms. Lady can I see you again
We have a future together and it's more than just friends
United we stand together I'm the Black God and you're my Earth
Loving each other increased the value of our combined self worth
I know I've found my treasure as I let the truth now be told

It's a woman called you and our loves stronger than
SOLID GOLD

YOU AND I

The concept of an unbridled love, self-sustaining and self- fulfilling independent but co-dependently existing came into fruition. At first, I was alone devoid of feeling, caring, love, its cousin's passion, affection and adoration. I existed in a purely physical state of carnality making bodies love me by use of my Divine rod that magically and seductively made women my tools. But that was before...
                        You and I
I see before you and I an endless stream of non-emotional involvements with the opposite sex, the sexual exploitation of a lustful God indulging himself, nay drowning himself in the sensuous wine of women who thought they had captured me by the grace of their charms and the fullness of their rumps or their swell of their breasts. However, none of them realized that they never had me until the scissors snapped marking the cut off point for the rocky ship of relations because they weren't you but I was still the I in I looking for...
                        You and I
I was still me seeking on this Earthly plane the object of my affection, the hammer that would break into my hardened heart, with loves forceful but welcoming persistence. I sought you I craved you on a level of esoteric proportions. I sought she who could be my woman, my soul mate, sharing an unspoken love language of communication. A touch, a look, a smile, ours would be a very special Love. For my Love was evasive and yet all inclusive. Beautiful but deadly and though my Love is free it must be earned. But no woman in that now is the time had worked hard enough for me to give it up and plus I was still looking for.....

You and I

You didn't see in the beginning how you inspired me to poetry of a romantic. How dazzled I was by your impressive beauty and ample womanly charms. And if you did see those things I'm sure you didn't know that I listened for and heard the silent whisperings of your heart proclaiming for now and forever more your undying devotion to me or the meeting of our souls on a metaphysical level as I stepped down from 7 to meet you on 6 and we discussed an eternity together. I had these discussions with you the first time I saw you underground in the East New York's Medina that is the Land of the Warriors. And as I was the warrior who won the battle on Love's battlefield surrendering myself and letting you into my loveless life. I gave love a chance to work because it was you for this I....

You and I

So much alike in many different ways, like two magnets of the same polarity repel away from each other we did also. But in my surrender, I gave a piece of me to you and whether you knew it or not accepting my piece with magnetic meant accepting the whole and I was determined to have all of you. I carried you in my mind and my thoughts would assemble a vision of you and right there in front of my eyes would be your face. See, I saw you when you weren't there and so I called your name, knowing for sure that I had found my own I love You and accepted.....

You and I

For me says it all. For years I have waited for your birth to the Earth discovering you in pants and now you're in the ¾ skirt. Behold me in all my magnificence for I am truly God of the universe, in which is found an understanding unifying relationship of Heavenly bodies our physicals are the one and one that makes three. So let's converse on

40

our level Man God and woman Earth because our love has been designed by Natures hand. And as it is so in the Universe so shall it be on Earth. This is our Bond, this is our Love this is our forever and always because you're the u for this I....
YOU AND I

WORD IS BOND DAY

Can precious love be measured like clocks count the hands of time
Are words inscribed in poetry beautiful because they rhyme
Can heavy heartfelt feelings be weighed upon a scale
Are thoughts I think delivered simply by the mail
Yes and No are two answers to questions in this prose
I write about a woman who for me is as sweet as a rose
To honor our relationship that we celebrate on this day
To love, cherish and honor each other in each and every way
So that we'll always remember and never forget
The years, months and days shared since the day we met
This marks our two year anniversary celebrating life
Peace Mei Earth Asya my beautiful earth and wife
You never have to worry nor doubt I will erase all fear
No matter who what when or why I'll always be there
For you offer me true comfort like shelter from a storm
Your love is like a blanket that keeps me soft and warm
Your presence on this planet provides for me a touch
Of heaven on earth and happiness that I need so much
So now we have each other and love is our tangible truth
That we are soul mates and our life together is our living proof
It can never be disputed you and I can never be denied
My love for you is heard and seen by all people with eyes

Our dedication is forever immortalized on the 27th of May
Commemorate and honor Born King Allah and MEA's 2nd
WORD IS BOND DAY!

BLEEDING HEART

How can I show it or give you a view
Of what's going on well first here's a clue
There's a pain in my chest something's broken in two
Inside the strong Black body that once made love to you
How can I say it, How can I start
To tell you the story of my Bleeding Heart
That use to be healthy all in one piece
We were so happy our love thing increased
We shared life and time together as one
But now I'm in pain and this hurt weighs a ton
How do I say it with a chest full of darts
That punctuates the story of my Bleeding heart
That cries red tears of lonely deep inside of me
Cause we don't talk and you don't even write Born King
You never gave me the reasons never explained anything
So now my pump muscles broken such agony it brings
Do I just say it or use my blood as paint for art
Drawing pictures telling stories of my Bleeding heart
That seeks to be forgiven a way to touch your soul
Like talk that bends your ear and lets my truth unfold
Do you remember loving me lovely like good women love their man
Think twice before crushing my heart already broken by your hand
How do I say it because now I've forever been marked
I can't erase the pain in the story of my **BLEEDING HEART**

NOT HE

You said that you could do it, you could hang out
But I know about beginning's I knew without a doubt
That after the beginning and way before the end
That you would be gone and called a fair weather friend
I know there's no difference call you girl woman or earth
In the end whatever the name you still bring the same hurt
But for the life of me I am still very strong
For I saw in advance that our thing would go wrong
It's like a prediction I wisely made in advance
But still i accepted the challenge to give you a chance
To tell me your lies, cheat and practice deceit
For sure I know now that our love took a back seat
To your stronger desire you know need for straight up sex
That drives you to forget me and instead you let your sex flex
You've submitted to the physical another mans dick
Excitement and curiosity both together helped you pick
The weak side of your nature and the arms of your man
But the reality is that you never really gave a damn
You hung around the true and living like a group sick groupie fan
Sucking up the life I give although you're barren land
So now I know I have been used and abused by you
But its partly my fault cause truly all along I've had clues
That I chose to ignore despite all the pleas
From my brothers in God and also a part of me

That I will never forget because internally I carried the pain
Of seeing you naked and fucking the next man in a porno inside my brain
So life is a lesson teacher for us all
I know I've been to class and will always stand tall
Regardless to what you do or fail to do for me
Cause I've learned to let you go you can now call me free
To start my life with someone else I know will be right for me
A mother to my children and true to me **NOT HE**

BLACK WISH

I wish that I may with all my might
To hold you in my arms and squeeze you tight
To stroke your hair and give your body delight
And make love with a passion to you all night
I'll start on your lips so sensual and full
Put my tongue in your mouth on your breasts I will pull
I'll put my lips around your nipples and start to suck
In the folds of your love my fingers will lay tucked
Gently I move my fingers as your hips start to buck
It's your body's natural reaction when you're ripe to be plucked
So out of your love comes my fingers hot wet and slick
As you prepare for the entrance of my big Black loving stick
Moans of pleasure escape you as your love lips open wide
As I have mounted your body and have begun to ride
It's a wondrous feelings to be inside your steamy womb
With the muscles of our bodies together keeping a sexual tune
I hit all four corners and touch bottom too
I tighten and tense and so do you
Cause a love well started is a love well done
As inside your luscious body my love juice shoots and runs
So in the afterglow of loves passion we lay back and insist
That what we shared was satisfying bonafide heavenly bliss
Because to me lovemaking begins with a kiss
But to make love in prison you'll need a **BLACK WISH**

I LOVE YOU

I've never forgotten my Allison her beautiful face full of charms

The pleasure filled days and nights she lay cuddled in my arms

She inspires me to poetry for her presence lives in my heart

That she'll always own a piece of for to me she's my work of art

Perfectly proportioned I loved her eyes, her lips, her breasts

My tongue is like a paint brush and my canvas was her love nest

She gave me so much pleasure though my world was full of pain

I see her through candy coated teardrops because she's my candy rain

But now I've come to see you in this a brand new year

To let you know that love never dies and to make it crystal clear

I understand you have a new baby and dudes a lucky guy

But he better treat you right cause you're Ms. Apple of my eye

Neither time nor distance or man could ever change this fact

That I got mad love for Allison McClean just know I've got your back

I'll be here for you to turn to although you've changed your name

On the strength of the past we shared I'm here for you just the same

Though we both are in relationship no disrespect I miss your love

So bad that when I rest at night it's you that I dream of

I have to tell you this that your constantly on my mind

On a scale from one to ten you're my one plus nine

I miss your pretty voice your sexy smile and creamy skin

From my mouth to your ears it's your heart I want to win

I want to hear I love you from you to me Born King

These three words are enough to make my broke heart sing

Absence makes the heart grow fonder, my love is grown anew

So this poem in so many words simply says that **I LOVE YOU**

USE ME

What is the difference between me and you
It's the things that I say and all the things that I do
From the beginning that never began I am
An innovative super creative Black original man
With a plan well put together like hands upon a clock
Tracks the passing of time with Mrs. Tick and Mr. Tock
My hands compose poems from the depths of my mind
To engrave my time spent wisely thought I'm caught in a bind
But what is left from the accumulation of days
That you spent in your prison, your addiction filled ways
Will speak for themselves louder than words
And make no mistakes you'll want to be heard
For man is a being who hurts, feels and cares
And pain is a luxury only the strong learn to bear
So I continue to take it one day at a time
To produces my thoughts in print that I can call mine
My direction and purpose is now mine to make
Success or failure I'll strive toward the good life gate
For I am greater then my faults, I work to destroy
Using the principles of Intelligence, I now employ
Steps and traditions form a ladder for success
To achievements, advancement and me at my best
The greatest potential of self is be all you can be
Has been released from within to be managed from A to Z
So my investment in tomorrow is created for all to see
I will always use my time and not allow time to **USE ME**

ANGIES POEM

Chocolate brown baby my sweet honey crème

I envision your presence your alive in my dreams

Oh how I've missed you but I'll never forget

Our moments spent together since the time we first met

Elite was the name of the Midtown Dance Club

That brought me together with my chocolate lady love

There was no preplanned action just the hand of fate

That first bought us together do you remember the date

With destiny I call it because nature sent you to me

So we could be together and start a family tree

A seed inside us was planted that had time to grow

And like a good farmer we get to reap what we sow

So now's the time to collect and harvest our rewards

Of a fruitful season of love healthy hearts can afford

I recall your thick as a snicker body dancing sensuously across the floor

The first time that I made love to you left me wanting more

Of your delicious nectar, Black woman you're a Queen

I heard a song call love jones and I know now what it means

To truly yearn for someone is sometimes quite a risk

You never know quite for sure if you too have been missed

But love is the power the strength that leads to a choice

And gives birth to the ability of my feelings to have a voice

Communication is essential how else could you know

My thoughts about you and how time has made them grow

Until they burst forth with this life all on their own

And are born complete with a name I call them
ANGIES POEM

YOU CARE

It's been quite some time, but I am happy to see
Words in a letter written by you to me
To reach out and touch me with care and concern
From the cradle to the grave we live and we learn
To pick and choose from the people we meet in this life
Who offer us true happiness instead of loneliness and strife
But even if that happens and we make the wrong choice
Somewhere along the line we'll hear reasons voice
Speaking clearly through confusion wisdom reaches ears
To endow us with the strength alleviate all our tears
Caused by pain and frustration that allows us to heal
Cause it washes away the hurt and prepares us again to feel
The full gamut of emotions we are now once again able to love
And be ready to be in a fit relationship like a hand inside a glove
My hearts been resurrected I no longer bear a cross
I've straightened out my life and told loneliness get lost
To find true love is unique and just so rare
I thank you Angie Marie and I'm so glad **YOU CARE**

WISDOM GOD DAY

Remember our loves pledge we made on the wisdom God day
Now it's a year later and we've grown 365 ways
We counted blessing deducting our troubles away
To bond us as one but we're two in love are the words we say
To allow us together to always hold fast
To the present we share and never let the past
Overshadow our vision and plans for tomorrow
Our loves for all time we conquer all sorrow
And live life in tune as we complement each other
As God and Earth we are natural born lovers
That took a step on this earthly terrain
To bond ourselves together for as long as we remain
Here on this planet that we've chosen for home
Although on this 1st year anniversary we are each alone
But nothing can stop us neither pleasure or pain
My love, have you ever dreamed of candy coated rain
Soul mates for real explains our inseparable way
And I love you even more now than I did on our
WISDOM GOD DAY

MS. YOU

Who is the girl who is better than the rest
Who is down in my book under B for the best
Who is known to give me much love unashamed
In my hall of fame I have written her name
It's you Black woman a young lady so nice
Who can share in my riches, my love and my life
A rich black treasure is the love we share
Its beyond comprehension even beyond compare
And now that I know it and sense that its here
This love revelation makes it all very clear
I want you I need you in more ways than one
I even want to bless you with our first born son
To love and to cherish whether for better or worse
My girl in the beginning but now you're my Earth
To have you to hold you for now and all time
You're my queen on this earth so regal and refined
Body in understanding culture for none are meant to see
Her underlying beauty is a sight saved for Mr. Me
She's the essence of femininity with beauty, grace and charm
Intelligently instructed this Black woman is known to drop bombs
To expand the conscious of many Ms. Lady has earned the right
Relationship with this man of the sun brightly reflecting his light
So the words written above are genuine and true
Sent through my loves hotline direct to **MS. YOU**

SWEET MOTHER OF MINE MRS. P

I know I've been talking about changing myself
To fulfilling my dreams to shower you with wealth
The kind you can welcome without any fear
So I ask you Dear Mother to cry no more tears
Your son has had time to remember your words
I wish I had listened to the advice I had heard
I wouldn't be here now stuck in this place
I didn't mean to hurt you or bring you disgrace
I was a hardheaded boy who unfortunately would learn
Pain in my life choosing the hard way to learn
The lessons you taught me I now know are true
So straight from my heart I sincerely thank you
For being a good mother to your bull headed son
For showing me tough love cause it needed to be done
For remembering my birthday and sending me a card
Loving me although I hurt you must have been hard
For keeping up my spirits, although I've let you down
For making me smile although I've made you frown
So for all these reasons I am changing my life
I want to come home I want children and a wife
Finally I've realized I have to change for me
And though it won't be easy I'll work hard to be free
Of the negative influences that captured your baby boy
Who now takes life serious cause you bring me joy
So now I am going to live life one day at a time
And give all thanks and praise to you **SWEET MOTHER OF MINE MRS. P**

BLEEDING HEART

How can I show it or give you a view

Of what's going on well first here's a clue

There's a pain in my chest something's broken in two

Inside the strong Black body that once made love to you

How can I say it, How can I start

To tell you the story of my Bleeding Heart

That use to be healthy all in one piece

We're so happy our love thing increased

We shared life and time together as one

But now I am in pain and this hurt weighs a ton

How do I say it with a chest full of darts

They punctuate the story of my Bleeding heart

That cries red tears of lonely deep inside of me

Cause we don't talk and you don't even write Born King

You never gave me the reasons never explained anything

So now my pump muscles broken such agony it brings

Do I just say it or use my blood as paint for art

Drawing the picture and story of my Bleeding heart

That seeks to be forgiven a way to touch your soul

Like talk that bends your ear and lets my truth unfold

Do you remember loving me lovely like good women love their man

Think twice before crushing my heart already broken by your hand

How do I say it because now I've forever been marked

I can't erase the pain in the story of my **BLEEDING HEART**

HAPPY BIRTHDAY

It's that time of the year when we add one more
Year and if we are lucky we get all the wiser for sure
That our time on this planet has been very well spent
In our years, months and days we've paid more than just rent
Investing in our future we're born of an endless race
Knowledge builds enrich the mind because it's a terrible thing to waste
But back to celebration cause Angie this poem is yours
Know that I think of you and just how you've touched my core
You're apart of this life that I live upon this Earth
Peace and blessing to the woman responsible for your birth
So every year on this date of August the twenty sixth
I'll remember that I chose a being that for me is a perfect mix
Special woman I am grateful for your presence in my life
Just talking to you baby eliminates tribulations erasing all my strife
Poems have been written many words have been said
To describe my feelings for you running through my head
Number one it's safe to say you have shown me love
Providing me with great happiness I use to only dream of
You're my chocolate passion fruit delectable and sweet
To know you granted me pleasure to have swept you off your feet
To shower you with attention, patience love and care
Much love to you soul mate it's your life I want to share

So my vision of Beauty may these words make you smile
And be welcomed in your heart for now but I'll be home in a while
To show you that I mean every word that I write and I say
So from the bottom of my heart, I treasure your
HAPPY BIRTHDAY!

PHYSICAL DAY

In keeping in tune with what is real
I control my thoughts when I write I feel
I'm opening a door to a inner world
In which the beat of my lonely heart unfurls
For within lies the essence of unadulterated truth
The ink on paper bears witness as proof
I love you Mei Earth Asya I write it in pain
A year has gone by its special time again
I've witnessed your growth from woman to earth
I've grown with you and recognized your wealth
Your value and beauty by you I've been blessed
I know our love can stand even tough times tests
As the planet keeps spinning age marches on
A year to every mile were just too right to be wrong
Your journey began in January on the twenty third
Your Book of life opened inscribing your first word
Seventeen years later destiny declared we'd meet
To have you in my world was a life expanding feat
With a nature so appealing I knew it had to be thee
BKA& MEA forever loving you changed me
Then as it is now into a man that you can love
For the better in every way you can possibly think of
Our future's what we make it lets shape it just like clay
Its heaven on Earth as together we too stay
So I give you me my will has found a way
To give you your props o

SWEET AS A ROSE

To my beautiful Black woman to my ebony queen
To my vision of beauty and the lady of my dreams
Yes it's the prince of power and the love of your life
Born King Allah writing poems that you like
To share my affection to make you all mine
Remember Black woman I am one of a kind
Because no one can do it exactly like I do
Making love was nothing till I made love with you
So now I still remember and you've got to forget the rest
Cause making love is nothing till you make love with the best
From the roundness of your rump to dimples when you grin
To the beauty of your hair to the texture of your skin
From the swell of your breasts and your delectable thighs
To the glimpse of your soul when I look in your eyes
All these things to me means that you matter the most
The most beautifullest girl in the world is my boast
Beyond the skin deep beauty lays an intelligent woman's brain
Her beauty is remarkable and Mei Earth Asya is her name
I want her with me forever one day at a time
Ninety nine years from now she'll still be my divine
I won't take her for granted she's earned my loyalty
The object of my affections there's no one else for me
I've realized her true value as the woman in my life
I'm true and living God she's the Earth and my natural born wife
I've got a total package from her head down to her toes

So I'll tell the world I love a woman who is as **SWEET AS A ROSE**

HEAD UP

No matter what keep your head up, even surrounded by despair loneliness and neglect caught up in a crossroads of existence where the only permanence is change. NO MATTER WHAT KEEP YOUR HEAD UP.

Because the tendency to look down due to the pressure of stress and anxiety is like an anvil on a rope worn like a two ton necklace of costume jewelry too cheap to give away. NO MATTER WHAT KEEP YOUR HEAD UP

To watch and maybe see that clouds of doubt though creating shadows don't necessarily have to rain on your parade because you can always take a rain check. NO MATTER WHAT KEEP YOUR HEAD UP

And then you'll learn that shit happens to fall on us and it's not all the time the pigeons fault shit head, I told you please don't squeeze the Charmin. NO MATTER WHAT KEEP YOUR HEAD UP

But you didn't listen did you so now something soft and smelly has landed like the stinking pilgrim on Plymouth rock. You've got oppressions shit heel on your hard head and now he lives in your brain. NO MATTER WHAT KEEP YOUR HEAD UP

And see just because you have shit for brains and think like a slave you can still see the light at the end of the tunnel that leads to the showers where you can get your brain washed. NO MATTER WHAT KEEP YOUR HEAD UP

And eyes open never hang your head in shame cause you can't see what I am saying, objects far away appear larger then what they really are. Don't settle for a rearview. Look the truth head on and don't let it pass you by. NO MATTER WHAT KEEP YOUR HEAD UP

For the truth shall set you free but freedom ain't free you must pay for the right to say I am somebody although nobody wants to their slaves go. After all you worked for free and still paid for a lie but still. NO MATTER WHAT KEEP YOUR HEAD UP

Because really where else can you keep it. Some people go through life with their head stuck up their ass always assuming for you and me as if being an asshole makes them an authority and you a toilet bowl, they can always talk shit too. NO MATTER WHAT KEEP YOUR HEAD UP

To receive the nutritional food for thought that enters the holes on either side of your heads face. Don't miss out being down get your earful of the sounds of these songs of freedom and come up; their all we never had, but now we do. NO MATTER WHAT KEEP YOUR HEAD UP

So that your newly found crown of intelligence can rest squarely on top of your cranium and never fall off. Because we learned **NO MATTER WHAT KEEP YOUR HEAD UP**

HINT

Who is this imposter who claims to be me, who jumped out the gate pen to pad using adjectives verbs and nouns, to assume my identity, thinking that his print would never be challenged he is foolishly mistaken.

You see you might be first out the gate but I'll never be late, cause I was first in the beginning and I'll be the last in the end. You see you're not profound, you're profoundly stupid, daring to construct an historical mirage, claiming the title of the true and living God when that is not you.

Your name is agent provocateur and though known for years you keep a low profile and write and bite like a plagiarist like you usually do until you are stopped and dropped with a mallet upside your head hammering home the fact no one escapes Justice Your pen cannot protect you and I know everyone has an opinion but like an asshole you continue to pontificate with impunity as if you have been granted bulletproof immunity.

How profound is the voice that like thunder makes such loud sound but it is the silence of lightening that will set your ass nay your soul on fire. For your eyes have seen the glory of the coming of the Lord and so you ran because you would have been exposed for the phony, fake, fraud that you are.

You need to be discredited because its given when its due and its half past the time for you to shut up. But no you won't will you ten percent keeps a sucker like you fang deep in the mentally poor who only saw what you appear to be not who you are. I can tell who you

66

are not you are not me. For I and the Father are one and you do not the works of my Fathers. I'm here to represent the truth untouched by your lies.
I am the 5% Nation of Gods and Earths recorder of time in print
So staple your thumbs together I suggest as a **HINT**

BORN BLACK

Who can question the complex order of life and created beings
The existence of immortal Gods remains a sight few have seen
The simplicity of a beginning that never has an end
The knowledge that tomorrow is just around the bend
Like a fork in the road of time to curved to see around
You imagine life among the stars but yet you live on the ground
Where natures wonders in abundance stated most emphatically
Life or death are both just facets of the same reality
Like a diamond goes unpolished or a pearl remains shelled in seas
The best in all the people goes beyond the body casing we can see
It's as complex as a spider's silken web connecting dots
When we as a people get it together the inner self rises up top
To the forefront of our conscious to the point where we must learn
The value of life in all its glory a priceless jewel we have earned
Take for instance a couple a pair each is one but together equal two
I for one must find the diamond in me to accept the pearl within you
For such is the way of the path to acceptance of life in reality
To self realization a womanly creation a relationship between you and me
But broader in scope is what's being written in this poetical form

And that's the strength of all beings to manifest true calm after the storm
To bring order from chaos, and peace out of war
To rise to infinite conscious from unconsciously closed doors
To bring healing from wounds and sunshine out of gloom
To rise respectfully but together I am Sun and you're my Moon
Living in the vastness of the universe our Earth spins at a terrific speed
The darkness is my identity from Darkness comes our family tree
In closing its my intention to state as a matter of fact
The true and living God and family are beings just
BORN BLACK

CHOSEN FEW

It's been some time now but still the truth must be told
Of the freedom loving Blackman who was wise but not yet old
Who radiated harmony and possessed a heart of gold
With his infinite degrees of knowledge the greatest to behold
The plain and simple truth is that he taught without fear
Allah's the God stop and listen that's why you've all got ears
But the old couldn't learn it the middle age didn't hear
Even some young fell to the pressure they caught from their peers
But A chosen few had listened and became a living part
Of a Nation undivided the Five Percent had made a start
Education is the basis to intelligence and we've made it a living art
We live to learn and it's no wonder our babies turn out so smart
It was 46 years ago when this truth to me was said
It's been my protection and insurance from the ranks of the living dead
I've made it my life and that's word is bond no longer astray can I be led
Cause the truth of Father Allah rests safe inside my head
Now I know that respect is given whenever it is due
And I see the truth in I when I see the Truth in you
Because self preservation was my first real clue

To becoming one of the righteous, one of Allah's
CHOSEN FEW

TRAPPED BY SEX

My poems have been trapped by Sex. Caught up in an overflowing cascade of emotionless digging, to find the proverbial pearl of wisdom hidden beneath the garments of a warm inviting but seductive suction of flesh, needing no words to express. My poems have been trapped by Sex.

I am gushing, no ejaculating ink from my pen upon blank paper never before wet with the ink of life for my poems have been trapped by Sex.

My conscious is in collusion with this unconscious act of prostitution giving myself, my poetry to sex for a fee that is never enough. And so I find myself walking the hoe stroll looking for my poem that has been trapped by Sex.

It is only now that I realize that I am piston pumped ready to fuck for the right to birth my poems into existence, but for now they lie in wait for the inter-dimensional door to open so they can transcend from mere thought into a voluptuous body of Poetry, for you see my poems have been trapped by Sex.

And what of this child my creation of androgynous ability able to transcend gender barriers in a single bound, blessed with the beauty of countless millenniums when in another form they swam in the darkness of a uterine canal searching for a home. My Poems have been trapped by Sex

And what came first the poetry or the Egg or is an idea spawned by man hatch its way into existence. Or is it the duplicity of my nature that made my poem say let go of my Egg O no twins please only I for you

see my Poems have been trapped by Sex
And now I am divorcing myself splitting in two, fours seemingly without Rhythm or rhyme but yet in tune with Natures call and the order became Law. But my Poems have been trapped Seeking to distinguish itself to make sense out of disorder, function out of chaos, a body out of solid liquid compound of oozing matter and long tail heads. My Poems have been trapped by Sex.

But slowly and surely creativity's compulsion to duplicate precision sculpted realties begins to assert itself and it grows arms and legs as extensions of its growth touching me kicking the shit out of me. My Poems have been trapped by Sex.

In an Embryonic Sac of Mystical Water breathable and drinkable able to withhold and sustain all at the same damn time, my Poem becomes I and demands to be free...But my Poems have been trapped by Sex

And there is no way out but the way in, but where's the path I cannot feel the floor. I am the little Baby Jesus walking on water for you see My Poems have been trapped by Sex.

Finally, an infinitesimal amount of Protoplasmic Energy has transcended celestial barriers metamorphosing its way to touchdown on a terrestrial globe rotating at a terrific speed of an Earthly nature...My poems have been trapped by Sex.

And now it is emerging showing its head downwardly spiraling outward trapped between two rock hard thighs and a three lipped nappy soft place, it's a tight place to be but there's no retreat...My Poems have been trapped by Sex.

So now I am just beginning to behold the Superlative Magnificence of the Embodiment of Creative genius that is rudely slapped into this reality from the next my Poems have been trapped by Sex.

So as the Primal Scream of Shock caused by the noxious inhalation of Hydro Oxidized gases are forced into two tiny workable lungs the breath of life is acknowledged. Light blinding images stifle the darkness of the Womb child that sees clearly now the rain is gone, but life goes on because this poems been born… but it's still true **MY POEMS HAVE BEEN TRAPPED BY SEX**

FOR I AM THE GREAT THINKER

Nestled in infinities cradle rocked gently by the Hands of time, I lie in wait for the opportunity to ride the stroller of material existence. To burst upon the Earth scene with the exuberance of virgin life in physical form I scream A.......L......L.....A....H, The breath of Life

FOR I AM THE GREAT THINKER
Contemplating the nature of Eternal life, I reach for the cosmos perhaps to find there the Origin of I the Original Man. But the cosmos in response behold me as a star within the Heavens descended upon Earth reply it was always U-N-I that we are brothers in antiquity, but it is u referring to I who is oldest and so with my hand upon my face held so because my elbow is lock positioned between my knee and chin in the repose of the Ancients contemplating the Enigma of Life I say Ummmm. The language of thought

FOR I AM THE GREAT THINKER
Traveling at a speed that only A alike minds can detect, I multiply positive thought infinitesimally upon the basis of Mathematically centered intelligence. The foundation to my house built on the existence of the true and living God is the greatest knowledge. My Black mind and body is produced from the thought I am, I was, and will always be. No beginning, No ending. I created creativity and exemplify extraordinary degrees of knowledge amplified through the wisdom of my sound. My voice possesses the power to raised the Dead mentally by touching the Brain stems of Blackmen seeking self in the midst of others. I say the Blackmans God is the first Principle of Intelligence

FOR I AM THE GREAT THINKER

But what of the slender Gender the X within my Y. who is Z and is Z she or He but back to her the bearer of my shine the reflection of my intelligence the object of my affections. My Nubian Queen my opposite entity sharing vast universes of time in motion with me. Is she not the most beautifullest creation in the world, nay the universe for it is from life and substance that she was molded to be of assistance to me as I continue to Pro- create and provide the means for little me and she's to enter through the dimensional door between there and here. She is the Natural earth the portal, the vehicle the soil in which seeds planted born great fruit through the wide opening of the X man now known as the wo-man. And as I lay with her head upon my beating heart I look in her face and see there the personification of Love and I say U. This is the Language of Happiness

FOR I AM THE GREAT THINKER

Once again alone seeking solitude in the fortification of my shell, my outer being body limbed number 5. Arm Leg Leg Arm Head but really 6 for am I not the two headed man? Without question I am the mental and physical progenitor of all known and unknown entities and bodies. But who is it that truly knows me inside my corporeal body. I have no definable structure I am energy boundless and ancient. Powerful and Productive for I am the Architect of Cohesive Thought that binds the I in eye to be the Born King of Kings and Lord of Lords. And in the end just like the beginning I am destined to once again be alone for I who was first will definitely be the last. So with the clarity of insight all I can say is I see ,for this is the Language of Understanding

FOR I AM THE GREAT THINKER

Endowed with the Greatest Responsibility, for all am I responsible as the Father of all Civilization, I am the God of the Universe whose thoughts transcended a

celestial form of existence conceiving the terrestrial Earth bound life encased in matter to show and prove I am, I was King and will always be Allah. Whatever I think I am for I am the source the Original Man Mind Intelligence superseding all barriers of time, motion and space for these are self created barriers. Self created but not for self, but for the energies other than self made imperfect through the thought of imperfection which bore bad fruit. And I saw it spoil and decay and die and so death and dying are processes that change matter and I don't mind. For eternal life is the privilege of only One who is I God and so to those who must end I say Good Riddance. For I am nestled in the Cradle of Infinity I gave you life and now I give you death. Responsibly I say Armageddon and I am going to get him. This is the language of Victory.
FOR I AM THE GREAT THINKER!

FREE THE LAND

What is this notion of mind blowing ever flowing, super conscious ability that supersedes ignorant miss-education and degenerative thinking in a single bound?

I am climbing upward to the sky to walk amongst the clouds with Air Nikes upon my feet, monetarily supporting the Corporate Welfare that spells my Defeat, I am the Superman to Man.

Without tights, capable of Walk flight, Dark as the Night, I resemble that unseen by the blind kind of Darkness that disguises itself as blue for with my X ray vision I see through you...Transparent Motherfuckers.

But this is only one of my powers for i am also Rain man as I shower your Brain cells with the torrential downpour of cascading Wisdom, Water, Oil for the brain retraining the thought patterns of the Dum, Dum, Dum, Dumb, to be all they can be instead of rusty replica's of their family Tree.

In reality their supposed to be like you and me, mentally free. But just like the sky is Blue the illusions still freezes thee at 32 degrees. I now ask if Ice is a solid, why is it wet? After this quiz there will be a test.

Given to those who i have come on my Intergalactic space body of Cosmic Origin spatially splitting the Atomic Law of $E=MC^2$ to become a solid made liquid,

as gas carries my sound to unbound those economically downed in Any Ghetto USA.
I am the Self Savior of Black people and I shout Freedom ain't Free it costs to be the boss. So go to the Head of the Class and pick up your test, Part One of your tasks is to study your past.

So again I ask What is this Notion of Mind blowing, Ever flowing Super conscious ability that supersedes ignorant miss-education and degenerative thinking in a single bound?......

Into the new Millennium we go. Melanated souls searching for truth in the muck and mire, of convoluted mixed messages. In Bibles, Qurans, Religious Schisms, Man Made Psychological Prisms, non-material Prisons.

While barbed wire insults continue to be heaped upon me by folks that don't look like us, but have convinced You that the Son of the Sky mirrors their reflection and Natural Selection is their claim to Racial Dominance and superiority in the world in which I am really the Majority. Fuck Darwin's story, I speak in allegory, Planet Earth is my House and they owe 6000 years back rent... Part Two of your task is you can now vent dissatisfaction about your present.....

TIME. So what I got a Watch, I know what time it is, Fuck a Swatch. Bet I know how to read History's clock. It's Half Past the time to kill the lies, Liars must die, so the righteous can multiply. Truth must be given Mouth to Ear necessitation, so the Ultimate Supreme of All Creation can assert his personal form of Cultivation, planting Seeds of Civilizations...Protected by the Red, the Black and the Green with a key Sissy.....

For your Puny locks, bars and fences are no longer defenses against Primordial awakened senses. For while you think I am locked out, I have locked in and you are the target. Dead man walking, while your body is the Bulls eye that I will not miss with my Marksman's gift. So stick your head up your ass and have a long kiss goodnight. Too Late, Too late Mr. Charlie bye bye NOW'S your time to go.

Where you came from go back for we no longer support your Hell on Earth. You Imperialistic, Capitalistic, Racist, Fascist, Communistic, Grafted Bastard. Your interpretation of how life should be for the masses of the Original Family Seeds has been tried, tested and been found untrue. But you don't have a clue what the revolution will do... Well, try these two words on for size DISCOMBOBULATE YOU!.... So now were at the finals part three of your test will be about the control of your future.

In which no needle or Suture will ever sow the seeds of your destruction again. Hear that all England's Kings Horses and all Americas Presidents Men will never put Euro-Centric Domination back together again. For African Centered Chocolate Covered Ebony Hued Auto-chones have known since the dawn of their Existence that Resistance beats the Persistence of the shallow Pink People who can't stand the Sun but must run to the shade, made in our image but can't really make the grade.

So fakes fail, Nature prevails, no longer do you rule this new school, new die has been cast. Testing, testing, 1,2,3, the Blackman has passed this class and kicked your ass back into its minute molecular structure.

So again I ask What is this notion of mind blowing

ever flowing, super conscious ability that supersedes ignorant miss-education and degenerative thinking in a single bound?

And at this particular juncture the answer to that First Question is........

The Notion has always been the Quintessential Power and Force called Change, that it is the Only Tangible Reality Sounds Strange. But it is Unimpeded, Unhampered, and Unrestrained. For it is, was and will remain a constant as in Always and Forever.

So it is quite Clever, Blacks who were lost have now come back to the source of life and thought. Intelligence borned itself a Son In Physical Form. Blacks began the journey of a thousand miles with one step, Jesus Wept, and I counted his tears as together we cried rivers and oceans; covering the Earth with Water. I am the Nubian Man who drinks from the Well of Wisdom with a gun and a plan until i have enough and raise my hand to FREE THE LAND.....FREE THE LAND....**FREE THE LAND!!**

MASTER OF THE GAME

I once read what I wrote had never been said

That life to a fool makes him the living dead

It's a sad commentary of modern day and times

You have 20/20 vision but the blind lead you blind

In a cloak of invisibility evil perpetrates its fraud

People worship the devil but always screaming good lord

But how can I tell you the words taught are lies

To trick you to fool you into wanting to die

For a people united these devils spawned crooks

Have beaten and killed us in the name of a book

Give us hell on this earth promising pie in the sky

As long as you slave and obey and never ask why

He's the first, the greatest the best and the last

Man I'm tired of this shit it's time to kick his ass

Impersonator to my people you don't represent the good

White supremacist America I now take off your hood

Revealing your pale mutated appearance and see through face

With your transparent intentions you proclaim superior race

Just like your Nazi cousins you're wicked by nature

All over the planet there are people that hate ya

By hate I won't be blinded I live for your judgment day

I got a righteous Black army so with your life you will pay

They'll be no hesitation see we're coming for your heads

With the sword our emblem of justice but today we'll fill you with lead

No matter the tool of destruction the end product is the same

You meet defeat at the hands of the one True
MASTER OF THE GAME

Made in the USA
Columbia, SC
19 September 2023